The Gingerbread Man

Key sound ay spellings: a, ai, ay, ey
Secondary sounds: ea, er, ite

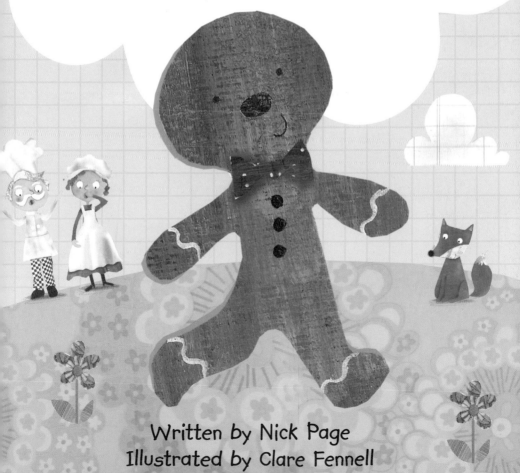

Written by Nick Page
Illustrated by Clare Fennell

There once was a crazy, old baker
and a crazy, old baker's wife,
and one day they made a gingerbread man,
who amazingly came to life!

The name that they gave him
was Gingerbread Fred
and they said, "Don't you wander away!
You are not a real boy, you're a pastry,
like the ones they serve in the café!"

But before you could say,

"CAKES AND BAGELS,"

Fred wouldn't obey – he ran off to play!

And Gingerbread Fred said . . .

"Run, run, run, as fast as you can,
you can't catch me,
I'm the gingerbread man!"

He made his way into a playground,
where a cat lay asleep by the gate.
"Oh, meow," said the cat.
"Here comes breakfast,
I wondered how long I should wait."

Meow!

But before you could say,
"CAKES AND BAGELS,"
Fred didn't delay,
but went on his way!

And Gingerbread Fred said . . .

9

"Run, run, run, as fast as you can,
you can't catch me,
I'm the gingerbread man!"

Next, Gingerbread Fred reached a farmyard,
where a dog lay asleep in the hay.
"Oh, BOW-WOW!" said the dog.
"Must be lunchtime!
It's a gingerbread-cake
takeaway!

Bow-wow!

But before you could say,
"CAKES AND BAGELS,"
Fred wouldn't remain,
but raced down the lane!

And Gingerbread Fred said . . .

"Run, run, run, as fast as you can,
you can't catch me,
I'm the gingerbread man!"

15

Then Gingerbread Fred reached the lakeside,

"Good day," said a fox by the bay.

"Need my aid?" said the fox. "I can take you.

You can ride on my back, just one way."

And before you could say,

"CAKES AND BAGELS,"

Fred was persuaded, and in the fox waded.

And Gingerbread Fred said . . .

"Run, run, run, as fast as you can,
you can't catch me,
I'm the gingerbread man!"

The fox said, "May I make a suggestion?"
as they made their way over the bay.
"If you stay on my nose, you'll be drier,
and avoid all this splashing and spray."

Good day!

Quite soon, they were over the water,
and Fred said, "Good day!
Thanks again!"

"Not so fast," said the fox,
"I've a brainwave,
would you like to fly,
just like a plane?"

21

And before you could say,

"CAKES AND BAGELS,"

with a cry of "wa-hey,"
Fred flew away!

And Gingerbread Fred said . . .

"Run, run, run, as fast as you can,
you can't catch me, I'm the . . ."

CRUNCH! SCRUNCH! MUNCH!
Fox ate him for lunch.

And Gingerbread Fred said . . .

Nothing. (Ever again.)

CRUNCH!
SCRUNCH!
MUNCH!

Key sound

There are several different groups of letters that make the **ay** sound. Practice them by helping Gingerbread Fred make some sentences. Use each word in the bagels in a different sentence.

they
convey
obey
survey
prey

baker made
ate lake came
lane persuade
race plane gave
take cake
gate bagel made
wave make

remain
rain
main
train
wait
aid
plain
brain

say
play
stay
day
spray
lay
delay
bay
playground
bay
replay
away

25

Letters together

Look at these groups of letters and say the sounds they make.

ea   **er**   **ite**

Follow the words that contain **ea** to help the baker find his bread.

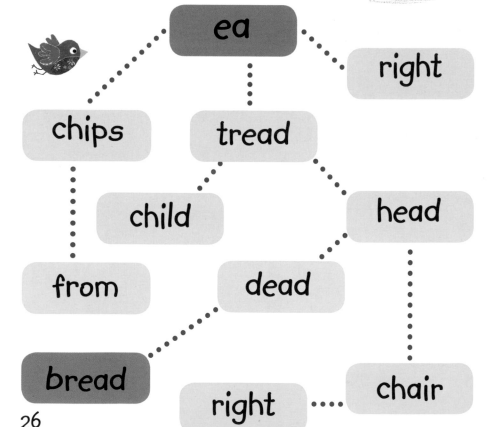

ea

right

chips

tread

child

head

from

dead

bread

right

chair

26

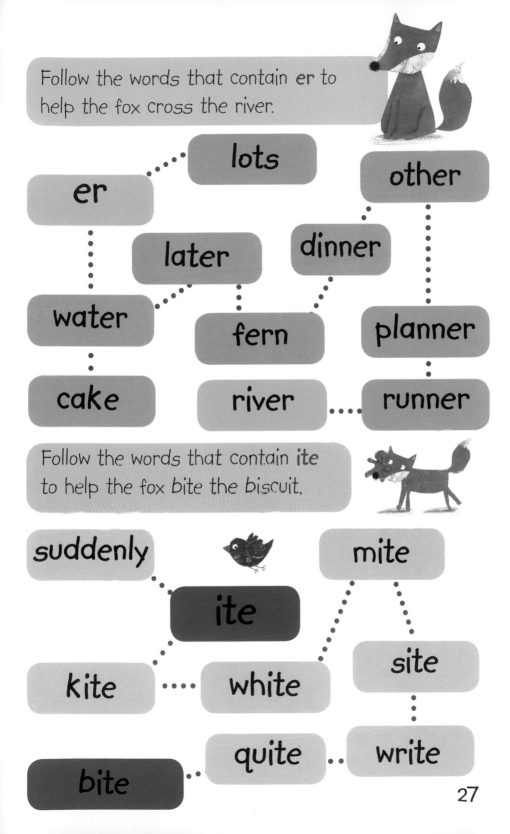

Follow the words that contain er to help the fox cross the river.

lots

er

other

later

dinner

water

fern

planner

cake

river

runner

Follow the words that contain ite to help the fox bite the biscuit.

suddenly

mite

ite

kite

white

site

bite

quite

write

27

Rhyming words

Read the words in the flowers and point to other words that rhyme with them.

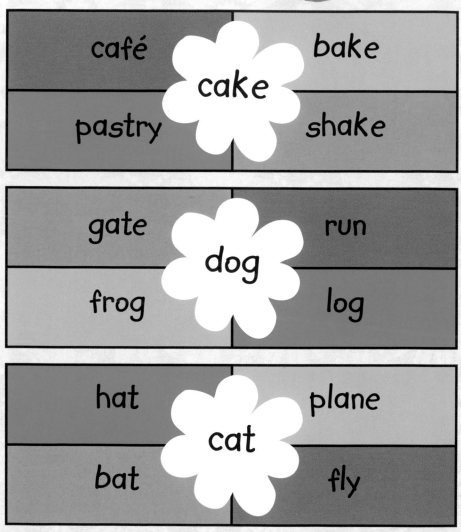

café

bake

cake

pastry

shake

gate

run

dog

frog

log

hat

plane

cat

bat

fly

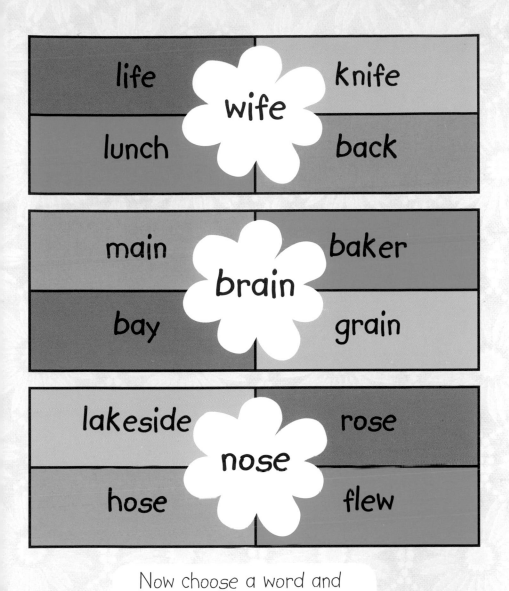

	wife	
life		knife
lunch		back

	brain	
main		baker
bay		grain

	nose	
lakeside		rose
hose		flew

Now choose a word and make up a rhyming chant!

The baker **bakes cakes** and **makes milkshakes**.

29

Sight words

Many common words can be difficult to sound out. Practice them by reading these sentences about the story. Now make more sentences using other sight words from around the border.

The fox ate Fred **for** lunch.

The cat and dog **couldn't** catch Fred.

The baker said to Fred, **"Don't** you wander away!"

The baker **made** a gingerbread man.

The **cat** chased Gingerbread Fred.

The gingerbread man **ran** from the baker.

something • animals • looked • got • it

• couldn't • town • a • sat • run • made • are • ran • we •